My Writing Book

by _____

Fill in your name

Created by Joyce C. Bumgardner
Illustrated by June Otani

SCHOLASTIC INC.

New York Toronto London Auckland Sydney

*This book is dedicated to CHILDREN,
with thanks to my cheerleaders,
young and younger.
SPECIAL thanks to Mary and Gary,
and to my student consultants:
Carolyn, Jason, Jennifer, Theresa,
Karen, Anna, Sarah, and Megan.*

ISBN 0-590-41785-1

Copyright © 1989 by Joyce C. Bumgardner.
All rights reserved. Published by Scholastic Inc.
Book design by Gina M. Iannozzi

12 11 10 9 8 7 6 5 4 3   1 2 3 4/9

Printed in the U.S.A.   23
First Scholastic printing, March 1989

You can write in this book!

Write stories . . . funny letters . . . important no-tices . . . secret thoughts . . .

Each page gives you an idea to write about. Choose any pages you like — you don't have to start at the beginning. Write a little or a lot.

Use your imagination! You may find yourself writing things you never thought you could write.

When you're finished, you will have your own book to read over and over again. You may even want to share some of it with your family and friends.

Just imagine! You have just come home from school. Sitting in your front yard is a HUGE, MYSTERIOUS BOX. It is bigger than a refrigerator, bigger than the front door of your school. A note on the box says, "OPEN SLOWLY AND VERY CAREFULLY." No one else is at home. It is up to YOU to open the box! How will you open it? What will you find inside?
(P.S. Strange noises are coming from inside the box!)

_____

_____

_____

_____

_____

Some things are SCARY, like goblins and witches, hailstorms and loud thunder, or finding a lion in your closet.

THINK of something VERY scary! Now write a story about it. Remember, it is YOUR scary thing, and you can do whatever you want with it!

_____

_____

_____

_____

_____

_____

_____

_____

_____

_____

_____

_____

_____

_____

HAPPY BIRTHDAY

One special thing that everyone has is his or her own special day. It is called a BIRTHDAY, because it is the day on which you were born.

When is YOUR birthday?

_____

How old are you now? _____

What do you like to do on your birthday? _____

_____

_____

_____

_____

_____

_____

_____

_____

_____

_____

What other special things have happened on the day that is your birthday? (You can ask a librarian for help, if you want.)

_____

_____

_____

_____

_____

What are some of your favorite things to do now?

_____

_____

_____

Ask someone to tell you about the day you were born. You might learn something new and special.

Put your school picture here ⟶

Not long ago, you were very small. Now you are bigger. You can do many things now that you couldn't do when you were smaller. WRITE about some of them. Tell what they are, and why you CAN do them now.

_____

_____

_____

_____

_____

_____

_____

_____

_____

_____

_____

_____

_____

_____

_____

_____

_____

_____

_____

_____

_____

_____

_____

_____

_____

_____

_____

_____

_____

_____

*Picture of you
when you were
smaller*

Some stories tell about magic lamps and about genies that grant wishes. If you could wish for just three things, what would they be? (You cannot wish for any extra wishes!) THINK VERY HARD before you begin to write. You have just three wishes!

_____

_____

_____

_____

_____

_____

_____

_____

_____

_____

_____

_____

_____

Winter, spring, summer, and fall—each season special things happen outside in nature. Each season you can do things outside that you do not do in other seasons. THINK of what you like to do best in each season.

Now WRITE about some things you especially like about

SPRING

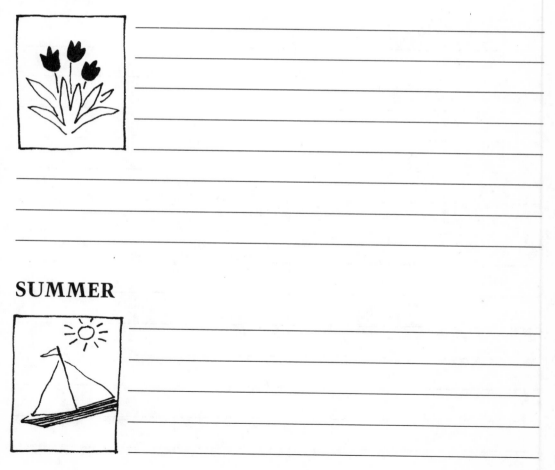

SUMMER

_____

_____

_____

FALL

_____

_____

_____

_____

_____

_____

_____

WINTER

_____

_____

_____

_____

_____

_____

_____

Sometimes, when rain is falling very hard and fast, people say it is raining CATS AND DOGS. Wouldn't that be funny! On a day when you don't like the weather, write your OWN forecast. Maybe it will soon be snowing white goosefeathers; YOU decide. For once, you can order just the kind of weather you would like!

_____

_____

_____

_____

_____

_____

_____

_____

_____

_____

_____

_____

When you open the door and go out of your house, you see and hear many things.

DO it!

Open your door and go outside. Find JUST ONE special thing and look at it very carefully. What is it? How BIG is it? Does it make SOUNDS? What COLOR is it? What SHAPE is it? Does it have a SMELL? Examine it very carefully.

Now go back inside. WRITE about the thing you chose. Tell everything you know about it. When you are finished, ask someone to read what you wrote. Can they "see" what you described after reading your description?

_____

_____

_____

_____

_____

_____

_____

_____

_____

_____

Some trees are very short and some are very tall. PRETEND that you are sitting in the very, very top of a tall, tall tree, looking down at what is around and below you. What do you SEE? How do you FEEL?

WRITE about it!

_____

_____

_____

_____

_____

_____

_____

_____

_____

_____

_____

_____

_____

Sometimes it is very nice to be home alone. You can RUN up and down the stairs and all through the house, and SING as loud as you want, and EAT all the cookies in the cookie jar!

WHAT DO YOU LIKE TO DO WHEN YOU ARE ALL ALONE?

Books are full of wonderful things! Sometimes you learn about new places from reading books. Sometimes you meet new friends in books. Sometimes you read about things that really happen; other times, you read about things that only happen in books.

THINK about a favorite book. Who is the author? What happened in the book? Why is it a favorite of yours?

Now WRITE about it. Maybe writing about it will make you want to read it again.

However old you are, you KNOW a lot of things! THINK about some of the things that you know, and WRITE about them.

I know that frogs can jump and swim.
I know that tiny popcorn kernels can pop wide open. Then I eat them!

I know _____

_____

_____

_____

_____

_____

_____

_____

_____

_____

_____

_____

_____

Fresh bread baking; warm chocolate cookies just out of the oven; the newly-washed earth after a rain; a favorite perfume or cologne; all of these are special smells.

What are some of your favorite smells? WRITE about them here.

_____

_____

_____

_____

_____

_____

_____

_____

_____

_____

_____

_____

_____

_____

There are many things that you might be when you grow up. Maybe you want to start thinking about it now. You might be a teacher, a radio announcer, a fishing guide, an engineer, or a pilot. You might be a forest ranger, a farmer, a doctor, or a computer programmer. THINK about it.

NOW WRITE ABOUT IT!

_____

_____

_____

_____

_____

_____

_____

_____

_____

_____

_____

_____

_____

_____

_____

_____

_____

_____

_____

_____

_____

_____

_____

_____

_____

_____

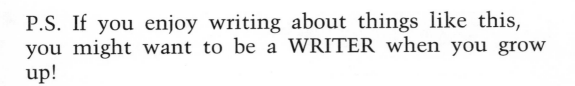

P.S. If you enjoy writing about things like this, you might want to be a WRITER when you grow up!

Inventors create new things that people need and want to use. YOU can be an inventor, too! WRITE about something that you think people need. What is it? How will it work? Why would people like to use it?

DRAW a picture of your invention here.

What is your favorite food? Is it a huge piece of cheesy pizza? Fluffy popcorn with lots of butter? Is it chocolate cake with lots of chocolate frosting? A big, crisp, red apple? THINK about it!

Now write a LETTER to your favorite kind of food. Tell it how much you like it, why it is your favorite food, and anything else you might want to say.

DEAR YUMMY _____,

Reporters often INTERVIEW people to learn new information. They ask questions, and then write about what they learn. YOU can be a reporter, too. Ask your mother or dad, your grandmother or grandfather, to tell you about the things they liked to do when they were your age. Ask about best friends, the house where they lived, their pets, their favorite games. You might want to take some notes while you do your interview.

NOW you can WRITE about what you learned.

_____

_____

_____

_____

_____

_____

_____

_____

_____

_____

_____

_____

Imagine this! You have just returned from having dinner with the prime minister of the Kingdom of Delicious. It was the tastiest meal you have ever eaten, served on dishes made of the finest crystal.

WRITE A LETTER TO THE COOK. Tell him how much you liked it, what part was the best and how you felt when you had finished this marvelous dinner.

P.S. Sometimes, if you write to tell a company that you really, REALLY liked what they made, they might answer your letter — or maybe even send you a free sample!

DEAR COOK,

_____

_____

_____

_____

_____

_____

_____

_____

_____

_____

_____

_____

_____

_____

_____

_____

_____

_____

_____

_____

_____

Sometimes it's necessary to apologize.
IMAGINE THIS: You have just returned from having lunch with the Queen of Kookamunga. Unfortunately, you knocked a big pot of cherry jam into her lap and it got all over her royal robes. When she tried to clean it off, she got it on her face and in her hair.

You got the giggles. You told her, "Thank you for the lunch," and left in a terrible hurry. Now you want to write her a letter of apology.

DEAR QUEEN,

Changing things can make you feel you've accomplished something. For example, you know that throwing bottles and cans and empty Styrofoam cups along the roads or in lakes causes POLLUTION. (When people do this, we call them LITTERBUGS. It is NOT good to be one of these!)

A good way to remind people to stop doing this and to help keep roadsides and lakes *clean* is to write a NOTICE about it and put it where others can see it.

WRITE A NOTICE ABOUT SOMETHING YOU WOULD LIKE TO CHANGE. Tell WHAT you want to change, WHY you want the change, and HOW you think it should be done.

NOTICE!   NOTICE!   NOTICE!   NOTICE!

_____

_____

_____

_____

_____

_____

_____

_____

_____

_____

_____

_____

_____

_____

_____

_____

_____

_____

If you could be an animal, what one would you choose? What would you eat? How would you get around? Where would you live? Who would be your friends? Where would you go in the winter? What would you do to stay cool during the hot summer? What color would you be? Would you have fur or feathers? Would you be big or small? THINK about it.

Now WRITE about it.

Each of us has a "secret me" inside. There are things you wish you could do, places you would like to go, ideas that nobody else knows. WRITE about the secret YOU. (When you are finished, you might want to paste a piece of paper over what you wrote, so it will still be a secret!)

_____

_____

_____

_____

_____

_____

_____

_____

_____

_____

_____

_____

_____

_____

Sometimes friends have to move away. Sometimes you have to move away. If this has happened to you, WRITE about it. Where did you move? Did you help to pack your family's things? How did you find new friends when you got to your new home? What could you do to help someone else who has just moved to your neighborhood?

(If you have never moved can you imagine how it would feel?)

_____

_____

_____

_____

_____

_____

_____

_____

_____

_____

_____

Money can be used for many things. It can buy the things you need and the things you want. It can pay for you to go traveling. It can be used to help other people.

IMAGINE that you have just been given a lot of money. THINK about what you might do with it. Now WRITE about what you might do.

_____

_____

_____

_____

_____

_____

_____

_____

_____

_____

_____

_____

_____

Just imagine!
One day while you are walking along the beach, a friendly gray whale swims up and invites you to climb on its back for a ride. You slip and slide as you climb onto your new friend. Then . . . .

WRITE about it. Where do you go? What do you see? What do you hear?

_____

_____

_____

_____

_____

_____

_____

_____

_____

_____

_____

_____

_____

_____

_____

_____

_____

_____

_____

_____

_____

How do you feel after you are back on dry land?

_____

_____

_____

_____

_____

_____

_____

Many people like to travel. Sometimes, so many things happen on a trip that you can't remember them all when the trip is over.

A good way to remember those exciting events is to keep a travel journal. In it, you can write the most important and special things that happen each day. If you write a little bit in a travel journal daily, it won't take much time at all.

WRITE about a real or pretend day of travel. Tell WHERE you went and WHAT you saw. Write about something unusual and different from what you usually see.

Painters make pictures with paints and brushes. Other artists use crayon, charcoal, and colored pencils to make pictures.

WRITERS make pictures, too. They use WORDS to make pictures.

THINK OF YOUR FAVORITE PLACE TO BE. Make a picture of it with WORDS. Tell WHERE it is, HOW you get there, WHAT it looks like, what SOUNDS you hear and what you SEE when you are there. What COLORS are there? How do you FEEL when you are there?

I like to be

_____

_____

_____

_____

_____

_____

_____

_____

_____

_____

Sometimes you have so many good writing ideas that you are afraid they'll disappear if you take time to write them in long sentences!

So that you won't forget any of your brilliant ideas, you can quickly make a list of <u>words</u> that will save your ideas. Then you can go back and write about them.

Example: <u>GARDENING</u>

I. Write just the <u>words</u> first.

garden
sun
digging
dirt
smells
seeds
shovel
rake
rock
rows
sticks
plant
birds
flowers
vegetables
soup

II. Then go back to the words and write sentences.

GARDENING

I love to be out in the **sun, digging** in my **garden.** When I dig into the black **dirt,** it **smells** fresh and new.

First I dig the dirt with my **shovel,** then I **rake** it smooth and take out all the **rocks.**

Then I **plant** tiny **seeds** that will grow into pretty **flowers** and delicious things to eat.

I plant long, straight **rows,** and fasten a string to **sticks** at each end so I can see where I made the rows.

While I am gardening, the **birds** watch and sing to me. I think they are happy, too, that soon there will be flowers to see and **vegetables** to eat! Then we will make my favorite vegetable **soup** and I will eat bowls and bowls and BOWLS of it!

Now YOU choose something! Maybe you will write about walking, or about roller skating, or playing soccer, or about making a snowman. Perhaps you want to write about your hobby. Turn the page and start writing. Remember, FIRST make your word list, THEN write your sentences.

LIST

_____

_____

_____

_____

_____

_____

_____

_____

_____

_____

_____

_____

_____

_____

_____

_____

_____

_____

_____

_____

SENTENCES

Famous people often write their MEMOIRS. (That's a fancy word that means the things they REMEMBER.)

You can write YOURS too! What do you REMEMBER? Think very, very hard of the *first* thing you can remember. WRITE about it here.

_____

_____

_____

_____

_____

_____

_____

_____

_____

Use this page to write a poem or a story.